Small Knight
and George
and the
Royal Chocolate Cake

To Phoenix,
a brave and faithful knight
R. A.

For Emma,
who ate all the chocolate
A. R.

ORCHARD BOOKS
338 Euston Road, London NW1 3BH
Orchard Books Australia
Level 17/207 Kent Street, Sydney, NSW 2000

First published in 2008 by Orchard Books
First published in paperback in 2009

ISBN: 978 1 84616 913 7

Text © Ronda Armitage 2008
Illustrations © Arthur Robins 2008

The rights of Ronda Armitage to be identified
as the author and of Arthur Robins to be identified
as the illustrator of this work have been asserted by
them in accordance with the Copyright, Designs
and Patents Act, 1988.

A CIP catalogue record for this book is
available from the British Library.

10 9 8 7 6 5 4 3

Printed in China

Orchard Books is a division
of Hachette Children's Books,
an Hachette UK company.

www.hachette.co.uk

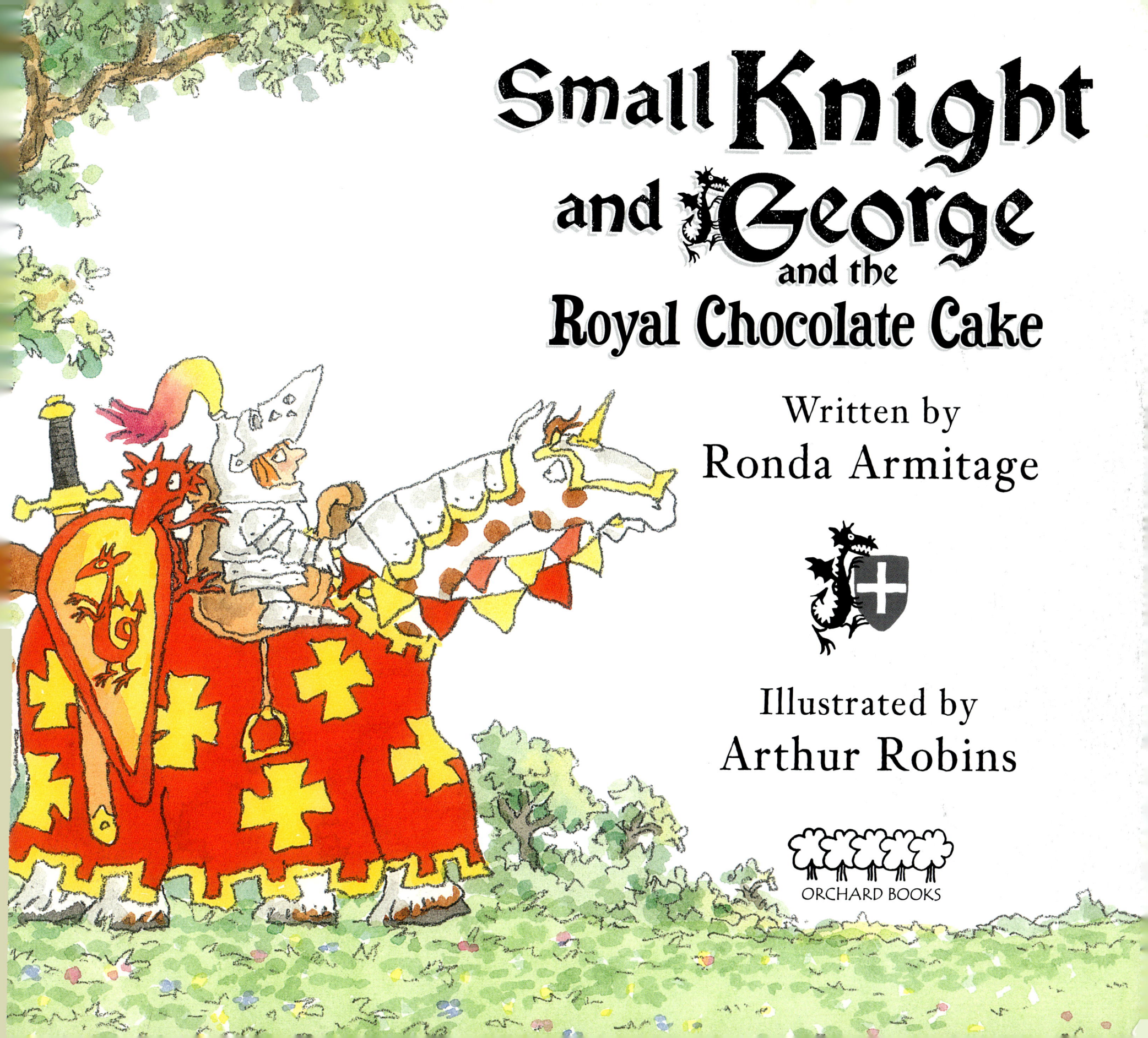

Small Knight and George and the Royal Chocolate Cake

Written by
Ronda Armitage

Illustrated by
Arthur Robins

ORCHARD BOOKS

MALL Knight and his friend, George, lived in an old castle on a spiky, high hill.

One morning, Small Knight received a very important letter from the King.

Dear Small Knight.
The Queen and I are coming for a Royal Visit.
Please invite everyone to a party and after could we play kick-a-ball?
Love from
King Wildred The Wonderful

P.S. The Queen says, please ask Big Cook if she would make her special chocolate cake.

BIG Cook was very
busy in the kitchen.
The delicious smell
of chocolate wafted through the
castle and out of the windows.

Mum and Dad Knight and
the ladies-in-waiting were
very busy in the castle.

Small Knight and George were
very busy giving party invitations
to everyone they saw.

THEY didn't see the wild brigands hiding in the dark, dark woods. The brigands were cross. "Nobody ever asks us to parties," they cried. The brigands were hungry. "We can smell chocolate cake."

In the middle of the night, while Small Knight and George were fast asleep, the brigands came.

Creep,
creep
on muddy feet.

They stole that
Royal Chocolate Cake
clean away.

"OH NO! Who has stolen the special Royal Chocolate Cake?" wailed Big Cook. "What will I give the King and Queen for the party?"

"Footprints here,
footprints there;
muddy footprints everywhere.
It's the
wild brigands!"
cried Dad Knight.

"Small Knight, put on your
armour, take up your shield
and your sword, and
get onto your horse.
You must find those brigands
and get that cake back."

Small Knight didn't want
to find any wild brigands.
He didn't even know
what brigands looked like.

"**B**RIGANDS hide in the dark, dark woods. They're wild and smelly and they steal things," explained Dad Knight. "You'll know them when you see them. You have to rescue the special Royal Chocolate Cake for the King and Queen. That's what brave knights do."

SMALL Knight didn't feel brave but he did like chocolate cake. He clattered in his armour and clunked in his boots.

He and George made up a song as they rode along:

"We are friends
    who are brave and true.
Today we have a job to do.
    To find those brigands
        and rescue that cake."

They came to the dark, dark woods. Something rustled in the bushes.

"Hello,"

called Small Knight.
"Is that the wild brigands?"
But it was only a wild
squirrel looking for acorns.

"I'm glad it wasn't the brigands,"
said Small Knight.

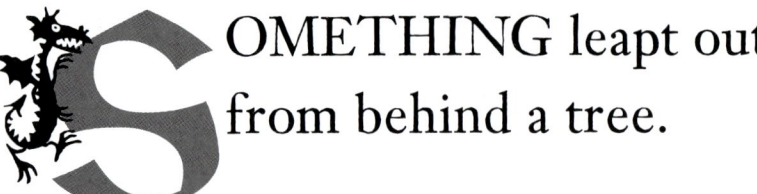OMETHING leapt out from behind a tree.

"Hello,"

called Small Knight.
"Is that the wild brigands?"

But it was only a wild deer
following the herd.

"I'm glad it wasn't the brigands," said Small Knight.

Something whooped and hollered in the dark, dark woods.

"Hello,"

whispered Small Knight.
"Is that the wild brigands?"

"Yes!"

roared the wild brigands.

"We're very **wild** and we're very **hungry!**

We just have to slice up this delicious chocolate cake and then we're going to eat it – every incy-wincy bit."

"Stop!"

shouted Small Knight.

"You must not eat that.

It's the very special
Chocolate Cake
for the Royal Party."

"Nobody invited us to the party," growled Bigger Brigand.

"And I'm starving!" cried Smallest Brigand.

"I HAVE to rescue the Royal Chocolate Cake for the King and Queen because that's what brave knights do," explained Small Knight. "But if you promise not to be wild then I'll invite you to the party. There will be lots of good things to eat . . ."

So, the brigands put on their best clothes, washed their filthy faces and brushed their wild hair.

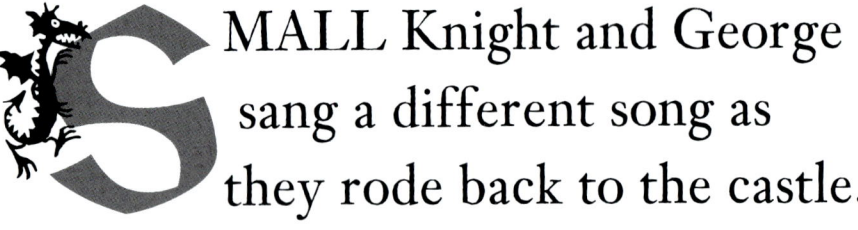 MALL Knight and George sang a different song as they rode back to the castle.

"We are friends who
are brave and true.

Today we had
a job to do.

The King and Queen
will cheer to see,

The Royal Cake
for the Royal Tea."

 **M**UM and Dad Knight were waiting on the drawbridge.

"Hello, Mum. Hello, Dad!" shouted Small Knight. "I've been a brave knight and I've rescued the special Royal Chocolate Cake."

"Hurray!" shouted everyone and they rushed the cake inside.

"**Watch out!**" cried Dad Knight. "Those wild brigands nearly caught you!"

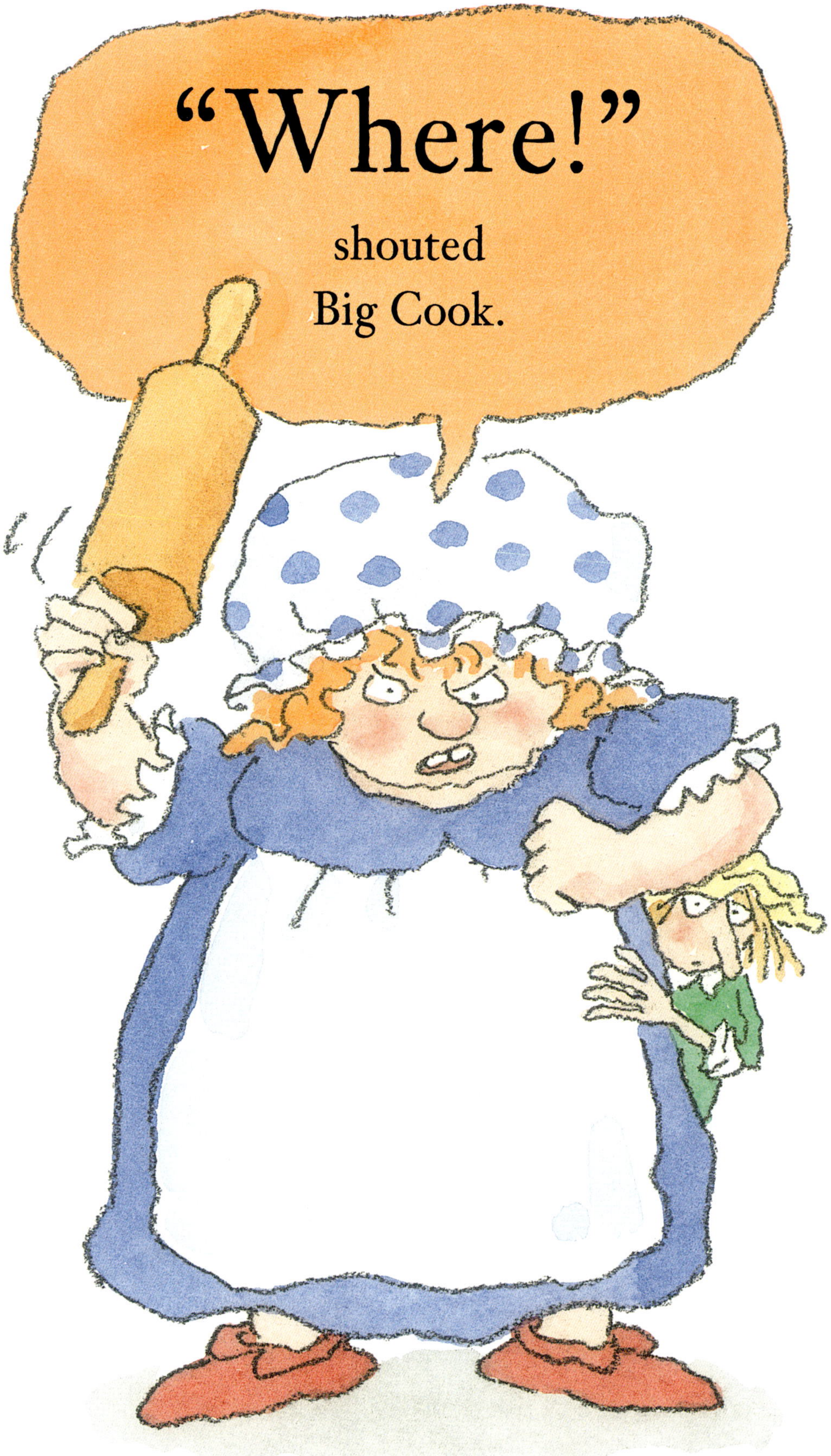
"Where!"
shouted
Big Cook.

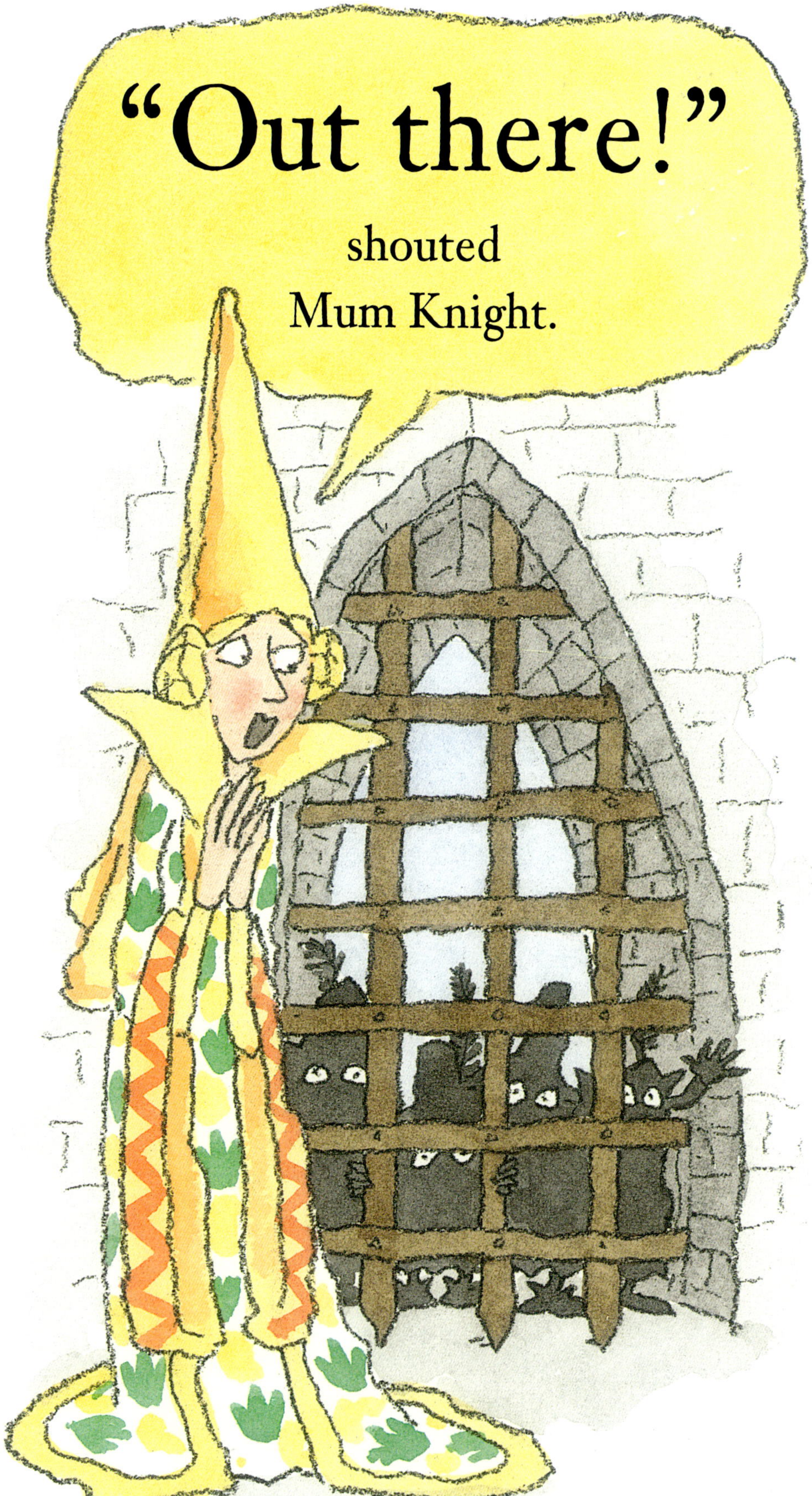
"Out there!"
shouted
Mum Knight.

"BUT they're not wild any more," explained Small Knight, "so I've invited them to the party."

Smallest Brigand began to cry. "I'm a very polite brigand now. Please may I come to the party?"

Dad Knight opened the portcullis. "I'm sorry," he said. "We thought you were still wild. Welcome to the party."

IT was a wonderful party.
The King and Queen
ate three slices each of the
special Royal Chocolate Cake.
The brigands were very well behaved.
They said 'please' and 'thank you' and
didn't talk with their mouths full.

Later they all played
kick-a-ball until it was dark.

"Thank you," said the
King and Queen and they
went home to their palace.

"THANK you," said the brigands and they went home to the wild, wild woods.

"Thank you," said Small Knight and George to each other and they went happily to bed.